AFGHANISTAN

BY HENRY GILFOND

AFGHANISTAN

FRANKLIN WATTS
New York/London/Sydney/Toronto/1980
A FIRST BOOK

Photographs courtesy of:
Steve Vidler/Leo de Wys, Inc.: pp. 6, 11, 25, 46, 49;
Victor Englebert/Leo de Wys, Inc.: pp. 16, 19, 30;
Rick Smolan/Contact/Leo de Wys, Inc.: p. 41;
David Burnett/Contact/Leo de Wys, Inc.: p. 54.

Cover photograph courtesy of Steve Vidler/Leo de Wys, Inc.
Map courtesy of Vantage Art, Inc.

Library of Congress Cataloging in Publication Data

Gilfond, Henry.
Afghanistan.

(A First book)
Bibliography: p.
Includes index.
SUMMARY: An introduction to the geography,
history, culture, agriculture, industry, and
current political situation of Afghanistan.
1. Afghanistan—Juvenile literature.
[1. Afghanistan] I. Title.
DS351.5.G54   958'.1   80–18356
ISBN 0-531-04157-3

CONTENTS

To the Memory of
my Father and Mother

THE DEMOCRATIC
REPUBLIC
OF AFGHANISTAN

Kabul (pronounced Cobble), the capital of the Democratic Republic of Afghanistan, is at least 4,000 years old, according to some historians. Archeologists are still not certain of the exact age of this ancient land. For thousands of years it was used by Europeans as a stopover on the trade route to China in the east and India in the south. It was invaded and held by Iranian tribes two thousand years before Christ. Cyrus, the Persian conqueror, ruled much of the land more than 500 years before Christ was born. Alexander the Great took over the Afghanistan region in 330 B.C. Other invaders came later, among them Turks, Arabs, Indians, and the Mongol hordes of Genghis Khan and Tamerlane.

Iran and India took turns at attempting to conquer Afghanistan in the eighteenth century. Then the British and Russians fought for control of the country in the nineteenth and early twentieth centuries. Recently, the Soviet Union, renewing an old ambition, invaded the land.

Invading Afghanistan, however, does not mean conquering the country. And if, as has happened frequently in the past, an invader has controlled the land for any length of time, he has never been able to hold it permanently.

The Afghans are a proud people. They are jealous of their freedom. They will fight with limited weapons against the greatest armies. They may lose battles, even wars, but they have never been utterly defeated. They have emerged from centuries of invasions and wars an independent people.

THE LAND

At one time Afghanistan included parts of present-day Pakistan, India, and the Soviet Union. Its present borders were set only about one hundred years ago, at a time when Russia and Great Britain were expanding their empires. Today, Afghanistan is not a very large country, with an area of 250,000 square miles (647,500 sq km).

It is a landlocked country, with no access to the open seas. It lies in South Central Asia with Iran on its west and the Soviet Union on the north. In the extreme northeast, Afghanistan borders the People's Republic of China. It is bordered by Pakistan in the south and the east.

West to east, Afghanistan measures 770 miles (1,240 km). From north to south its greatest width is 550 miles (880 km). On a map, it looks very much like an irregularly shaped leaf. The Hindu Kush, a towering range of mountains, runs through the middle of the country, northeast to southwest, separating the rich soils of the northern plains of Afghanistan from its deserts in the south. The central part of the country consists of

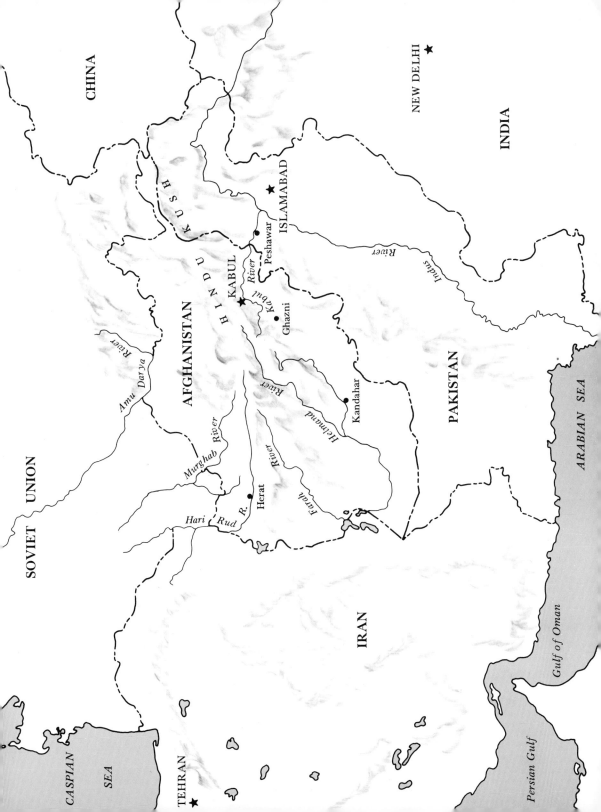

fertile valleys and stretches of grasslands among the highlands.

The whole country may be seen as divided into four geographical areas. The Hindu Kush and its smaller ranges of mountains run through the middle of the country from northeast to southwest. The foothills of these ranges, generally arid with practically no vegetation, is the second area. Sloping plains and steppes, watered by the rivers flowing from the mountains in the northern regions, constitute the third area of Afghanistan. The fourth area, the south and particularly the southwest, is all desert and wasteland.

Only one river in Afghanistan, the Kabul, reaches the sea. The Kabul River flows beyond the Afghan borders into Pakistan, where it is known as the Indus, and then into the Arabian Sea. The Amu Darya River, about 700 miles (1,120 km) long, forms a border between the Soviet Union and Afghanistan. Other principal rivers in Afghanistan include the Helmand, about 700 miles (1,120 km) long; the Hari Rud River, about 650 miles (1,040 km) long; and the Murghab and Farah rivers, each about 400 miles (640 km) long. None of these rivers is used for shipping, but they do serve to water the fertile lands of the country.

Afghanistan is parallel on the globe with Texas, but its climate and weather are quite different. Texas does not have the mountainous areas that cover so much of the Afghan country. The climate of Afghanistan is continental, with very hot summers and very cold winters. The Afghans experience great changes in temperature between night and day. There is snow in the mountains for ten months of the year, and it may be very hot in the sun during the day, but very cold at night. Winds in the mountains sometimes reach a velocity of 110 miles (176 km) an hour, and blow great dust storms into the plains.

The valleys have less dramatic weather. They get a moderate amount of snow from November to April. Summer months are cloudy and hot, but the nights are cool. In Kabul, for example, the average daytime temperature almost never falls below freezing, and rarely rises beyond a comfortable spring temperature.

VEGETATION

The vegetation in Afghanistan is as varied as the country's landscape. There are forests of tall pine and fir trees in its highest mountains, as well as oaks, yews, and cedars. Near the base of the mountains, there are walnut trees, wild almond, and myrtle. In the higher reaches of the mountains, wild olive, privet, hazel, larch, pistachio, and Judas trees are abundant, as well as the Norway spruce and the wild peach in certain areas. At lower altitudes, alder, ash, arbor vitae, juniper, and a variety of other trees are plentiful.

Various bushes, protected by these trees in the lower areas of the mountains, give the Afghans a variety of currants, gooseberry, hawthorne, honeysuckle, jasmine, rose, and rhododendron. Where the hills are drier, there is a thin growth of a variety of herbs and thorny plants: milk vetch, rhubarb, rue, wormwood, and camelthorn.

On the steppes, with the advent of spring, there is a carpet of grass and a multitude of flowers, including tulips, lilies, daffodils, irises, hyacinths, and wild roses.

The forests of the extreme northeast of Afghanistan provide considerable timber, resin, and asafetida (which once was used for medicines). They also provide enough pistachio and pine

*Downtown Kabul is a blend of old and new as
merchants walk their produce-laden donkeys
past the cars and modern buildings of the city.*

nuts to export to other countries. The Afghans cultivate ash, mulberry, poplar, and willow trees both for their yield in wood and for shade. The mulberry is also cultivated because its leaves are needed in the manufacture of silk, and because its berries, both fresh and dried, are a staple food, particularly in the area north of Kabul.

The Afghans also cultivate orchards of peaches, apricots, pears, almonds, walnuts, and apples, much of which is exported. Date palms are cultivated in the extreme south, and melons and cucumbers are grown wherever possible. Where the weather is warm enough, the Afghans grow oranges and pomegranates.

The main crops of Afghanistan, grown on all fertile lands, are wheat, barley, rice, corn, millet, sesame, and vegetables. The Afghans also grow opium poppies, the plants from which codeine, morphine, and heroin are produced. Sugarcane, sugar beets, and turmeric are among the other important crops. Flowers, too, are grown wherever possible, for the brilliance and the cheer they give their houses and gardens.

Obviously, Afghanistan does not lack vegetation. Reeds and rushes grow in its marshes. Even in its desert regions, there are stunted brushwood, dwarf tamarisk, camelthorn, asafetida, and gum trees from which the Afghans get tragacanth, a gum used for adhesives and for textile printing.

ANIMAL LIFE

Tigers, once common in Afghanistan, have been killed by hunters to the point that they have all but disappeared. They are still seen on occasion, however, in the remote mountain areas. Smaller wild animals are still in abundance. There are wild goats and sheep, ibex, bears, wolves, foxes, jackals, and gazelles. Wild bird life is plentiful, too, and there are vultures in great number.

Camels, horses, donkeys, cattle, and yaks are the principal domestic animals in Afghanistan. Water buffaloes are yoked to tread out the wheat harvest. Cattle are used as work animals, too, as well as to provide milk. Camels, horses, and donkeys are used as beasts of burden as well as a means for transportation. Afghans are particularly proud of their horses. The more horses a man has the more he is respected by his community.

Karakul sheep and fat-tailed sheep are especially important to the Afghans. They herd millions of them, and karakul hides are among the chief exports of Afghanistan.

Finally, there is a ferocious Afghan dog, called kuchi, that sometimes grows as big as a small mule. It is used as a sheep dog and will attack a wolf, fox, or human being on sight. But, at the same time, it is a magnificent shepherd and most faithful to its master.

CITIES

Afghanistan's important cities —Kabul, Kandahar, Ghazni, and Herat—have remained comparatively unchanged over the centuries. There are, however, some relatively tall, modern buildings, particularly in the capital city of Kabul. There are automobiles and some paved, wide streets. Many of the people wear western-style clothes. But the ancient city walls are still in evidence. Most streets are narrow, winding, and unpaved. Camels, donkeys, horsemen, and occasional flocks of sheep make up most of the traffic. Sacred Muslim mosques are everywhere. In the bazaars, merchants and shoppers still conduct business in the ways of their ancestors. Most men wear the ancient Muslim baggy trousers, long shirt, and turban; and the women, for the most part, do not go outdoors without wearing their *chadris*, a veil that covers the entire body from head to toe except for the eyes, as required by Muslim religious law.

The buildings in the cities are mostly constructed with mud and unbaked brick. High mud walls, locked doors, and barred windows secure privacy for the Afghans and, in the custom of the Muslim world, keep their women out of public sight.

[9]

KABUL

Two craggy mountain ranges surround this ancient city that has been the capital of Afghanistan since 1776. The Kabul River flows through a narrow pass between these two ranges and meanders through the heart of the city. Bala Hisar, a citadel centuries old, dominates the landscape of Kabul. The ancient walls of the city, believed to have been built in the fifth century, are 23 feet (7 m) high and ten feet (3 m) thick.

Some of the older sections of Kabul have been demolished and have given way to broad streets, shops, and other places of business. Textile merchants, vendors of spices, carpet sellers, jewelers, and leatherworkers crowd the bazaars. There are teahouses and cafés in great number.

In the newer section of the capital, which the Afghans call "Shar-i-No" (new city), is the People's House, the palace of former rulers of Afghanistan. Government buildings are here, as are the foreign embassies, banks, hotels, the schools, and colleges. Here, the wide streets are paved and lined with trees. There are villas and comfortable homes in this section, too, but only a few are visible from the streets. They are almost all surrounded by gardens and hidden from view by high walls. More than one hundred mosques dot the city everywhere.

At a bazaar in Kabul, men barter with women covered from head to foot in chadris.

KANDAHAR

The history of this Afghan city goes back to Alexander the Great, more than 2,300 years ago. The city Kandahar was originally named for him.

About one hundred years after Alexander, the entire area around Kandahar became known as Gandhara and was ruled by Buddhists from India. In the early 1500s, another conqueror, Babur, who claimed to be descended from Genghis Khan, carved a monument to himself in stone in Kandahar. Forty steps in the mountainside lead to a chamber carved into the mountain. Inside the chamber there is an inscription stating that this monument was built by Babur, founder of the Mogul Empire, and listing all the lands over which he ruled. The monument is called Chel Zina and still stands today.

The Kherqa Sharif, in Kandahar, is one of the most sacred shrines in Afghanistan. It contains a cloak that is believed to have belonged to the Muslim prophet Mohammed. The relic was brought to Kandahar in 1747 by Ahmad Shah Sadozai, under whose leadership the Moguls were driven out of Afghanistan.

As with Kabul, Kandahar has both a "new city" with paved streets and an "old city," with narrow, winding, unpaved streets and bazaars. The mullahs—religious leaders and teachers—were until the Soviet invasion particularly powerful in Kandahar and sometimes militantly prevented western ideas and customs from entering the life of the people of this ancient city.

HERAT

No one knows exactly how old this city on the Hari Rud River is. It was old before the Persians took it into their empire and before Alexander the Great moved into Afghanistan. It is directly on a road that leads from Persia (Iran) to India and it was constantly attacked, taken, and destroyed by conquering armies. It was rebuilt after one such destruction by Alexander the Great.

The wall surrounding the city, erected when it was known as Aria, in ancient times, is a mile (1.6 km) long. But it proved no defense against the many different hordes that invaded Herat. Nor was the fort that Alexander built a major deterrent to invading forces. Alexander's citadel, incidentally, still stands and dominates the landscape of Herat.

Herat was once a great seat of learning with magnificent mosques. The beautiful Musalla complex, built in the late 1400s, consisted of a striking madrassa (place of learning) and an equally striking musalla (place of worship). All that remains of this structure, however, are six of the twelve minarets (towers) that originally flanked the buildings.

Learned people, and particularly poets, were highly esteemed in old Herat. The tomb of Gazargah, an eleventh-century poet, was restored by the Shah Rukh in 1428 and still stands. A carefully tended pistachio tree grows from the tomb of Jami, a fifteenth-century poet of Herat.

As everywhere in Afghanistan, there are any number of mosques and well-kept shrines. The most famous mosque in Herat is the Masjidi Jami. It stands in the middle of the city and has been rebuilt many times. At this site in the city there has been a place of worship for different faiths as far back as the times of Zoroaster, the Persian prophet of the sixth century before Christ.

Commercially, Herat is bustling with textile weaving and the making of carpets, in addition to all the usual activities of the bazaars in Afghanistan. And because of its abundance of flowers, it is one of the most beautiful garden spots in the country.

GHAZNI

Ghazni was the greatest city in Afghanistan some thousand years ago, when it was the capital of the country. It was ruled at the time by the Turks, whose empire then encompassed parts of northern India, Persia, and Central Asia. The empire fell, however, and Genghis Khan and his horde destroyed everything of value in Ghazni, in 1221.

Ghazni has never recovered the importance and grandeur of its past, with its splendid palaces and mosques, when it was the home of many artists and writers, including Firdawsi who has been called the "Persian Homer," after the greatest of all writers of epic poetry. It remains, however, strategic to the economy of the country. It is on the direct route that connects Kabul with Kandahar and then goes on to Herat. Ghazni is the home of one of Afghanistan's more important markets. It is also the staging point for nomads moving to and from the Indus Plains of Pakistan.

Ruins abound in the cities of Afghanistan, reminders of long-ago inhabitants and former glory. The Afghans have attempted some restoration of these ruins, particularly those that are part of the Muslim culture. But restoration is a costly process and Afghanistan is a poor country. Many of the ruins, spelling out the history of Afghanistan, remain untouched, except by the winds, the rains, and the snows, as well as the sandstorms, that slowly wear down these ancient relics.

THE PEOPLES
OF AFGHANISTAN

As is the case with many other countries in the world, no one knows who the original inhabitants of Afghanistan were. Two thousand years before Christ, Aryan tribes moving through the Hindu Kush, probably on their way to the fertile soils of India, encountered a land inhabited by Dravidians and people of an even older race. Dravidians occupied India at one time, before the coming of the Aryans, and still do to a large extent. There is nothing, to date, which tells us anything of that older race that lived in Afghanistan.

A few centuries after the Aryans, the Persians moved into Afghanistan. Then came the Scythians, probably out of the Black Sea regions; then the Baluchi out of Pakistan; and a host of other tribes out of Central Asia.

The Turks pushed into Afghanistan in the seventh century. The Mongols surged into Afghanistan in the thirteenth century. In the fifteenth century, the Turko-Mongol Uzbeks moved in great numbers into the country.

*An Afghan nomad leads his camels across
the plains of north central Afghanistan.*

Today, there are at least sixteen ethnic groups among the 18 million people (2.5 million of them nomads) that inhabit Afghanistan. And each of the sixteen ethnic groups consists of a large number of separate but related tribes. There are also the descendants of the Greeks, Arabs, Turks, and a variety of Mongols who remained in Afghanistan, as the different reigns of their leaders came to an end.

Just as immigrants of all times tend to find a home among people of the land from which they came, the various tribes that came into Afghanistan built their enclaves in areas of the land which suited them best.

The Turko-Mongol peoples settled in the northern regions of Afghanistan, the Hazara in the central part of the country. The Pushtun people settled in the south, the Tajik in the northeast. The Kafirs, later called Nuristani, made their home in the northeast as well.

About 60 percent of Afghanistan's population are Pushtuns. We have yet to discover the origin of these people, but we do know that they are a mixture of many different clans and tribes. A great number of Pushtuns are highly educated, and live and work in Afghanistan's cities and towns. Certain tribes among the Pushtuns prefer village life and farming, though they are known to return to a nomadic way of living and to move out of their villages and dwell in tents during the summer months. Other Pushtun tribes are content to plant just a few crops, then go off with their flocks to pasture. Finally, there are a few Pushtun clans who live by raiding merchant caravans and by robbing people who refuse to pay for "protection." The Pushtun people are as varied as their different tribes, and each tribe lives according to its own customs.

[17]

The Tajiks constitute about 30 percent of the population of Afghanistan. They may be the descendants of the first Iranians in Afghanistan. Or they may be the descendants of the Arabs who had conquered Iran.

There are roughly two separate groups among the Tajiks. The Tajiks who are village-dwelling farmers in the mountainous areas of Afghanistan are an extremely poor people. Their language is Dari, an archaic dialect of Farsi, or Persian.

The second group of Tajiks are town dwellers. They are farmers, too, but they are also skilled craftspeople and tradespeople. They can be found in every bazaar and wherever goods are bought and sold. Their language is very much like the language of eastern Iran.

The Uzbeks, about 5 percent of the Afghan people, were originally nomads, but they have become village dwellers, farmers, and tradespeople. The Uzbeks intermarried with the Tajiks and adopted their way of life and their customs, but they continued to speak their Turkic language. However, when they are involved in a business deal, in town, they speak Dari, one of the two official languages in Afghanistan. (The other official language is Pushto.)

Hazara Mongols live in Hazarajat, in the central part of Afghanistan, and around Herat, on land that is not very fertile.

This young nomad boy leads a life of continual travel, moving with his tribe and its cattle from one grazing area to another.

[18]

Their fortified villages of mud or stone houses are set at the edge of valleys, where they grow barley, wheat, and peas. They also graze sheep on the slopes that rise from the valleys. Their language is described, too, as Dari, like that of the mountain-dwelling Tajiks, but many of the words they use are Turkish and Mongol.

The Nuristani tribes, sometimes called Kafirs, claim descent from the Arabs but are more likely remnants of the original people of Afghanistan. They herd goats and cattle in the northeastern mountains of the country, where they live in two- or three-story wooden houses with ornamented upper verandas. Until recently, they sacrificed cows and goats to their gods.

In the far northern tip of the country are the nomad Kirghiz. North of the Hindu Kush are the Yueh-chi. In the south are the Kalaj Turks. Turkomans live in dome-shaped tents on the border of the Soviet Union. The Baluchi people live in black tents on the Iran border.

In all, there are more than twenty languages spoken by the almost countless number of tribes and clans who make up the population of Afghanistan. But fully 80 percent of these people speak one of two languages. Dari is the dominant language in the capital of the country, and is spoken and understood by many people in every town of any size. Pushto is the dominant language in Kandahar.

Despite the differences of origin and language, however, there is much that is common to the peoples of Afghanistan. For the most part they were all originally agricultural people, and those who were not, the nomads, eventually settled down to till their own lands.

As a people, the Afghans are unusually hospitable to visitors, but their tribal background and the many wars they have suffered often make them suspicious of strangers and foreigners.

Most Afghans are poor, but they are a markedly independent and proud people. Family pride and prestige, loyalty, piety, and courage are more important to them than the possession of automobiles, refrigerators, televisions, and other material goods. They may consider new ideas, but only if such ideas do not conflict with their religion and traditions. Nothing is more important to Afghans than their religion, Islam, and the traditions of their ancestors.

ISLAM:
A WAY OF LIFE

The official religion of Afghanistan is Islam, but the faiths of Jews and Christians are tolerated. The Hindus, Moslems believe, worship idols.

The few thousand Hindus who live in Afghanistan are shopkeepers, merchants, and herb doctors. The Jewish communities in Kabul and Herat are quite small. Kabul is the home, too, of a small number of Zoroastrians whose scriptures are contained in the Avesta, their holy book that promises the coming of a messiah. The only Christians in Afghanistan are the members of foreign embassies and legations, and representatives of European and American business interests.

At the time of the Soviet invasion, about 99 percent of the Afghan population was Muslim. The great majority of the Muslims, 80 percent, belong to the Sunni sect of Islam. This is considered the orthodox sect and most of the rulers of Afghanistan have been Sunni.

The Shia sect of Islam constitutes about 18 percent of the people. They believe that the spiritual leadership of the Muslim world descends from Ali, the son-in-law of the prophet Mohammed.

Both Shiites and Sunnis endorse the "five pillars" of Islam to which all Muslims must adhere:

1. A Muslim must say, at least once a day, "There is no god but Allah, and Mohammed is his prophet."

2. He must pray five times a day: at dawn, at noon, in the mid-afternoon, at sunset, and after nightfall. He must wash himself before he prays, cover his head, take off his shoes, and kneel on a carpet. He must face Mecca, the birthplace of Mohammed, as he prays, bow and prostrate himself, in turn, continually until his prayers are done.

3. He must be charitable to the needy.

4. He must fast during Ramadan, the ninth month in the Muslim calendar, the month in which the Koran was sent down to Mohammed. The only ones exempt from fasting are the physically weak, the sick, and soldiers. According to Muslim belief, the gates of paradise are open during Ramadan, the gates of hell shut, and the devils in chains. During the entire month, the faithful must fast from sunrise to dusk.

5. If possible, once in his lifetime, he should make a pilgrimage (hajj) to Mecca.

The Koran is the holy book of Islam. Like the Bible, it calls on the faithful not to sin. It is a sin for Muslims to eat pork or drink alcoholic beverages. Other sins are much like the sins to be avoided by Christians and Jews.

[23]

When a Muslim prays he does not petition Allah (the god of Islam) for any gifts or special requests. He limits himself to praising Allah, adoring him, and thanking him for his blessings.

The Koran, incidentally, considers Abraham, the father of the Hebrew people, to be the first Muslim. They believe, with Christians, that Jesus was born to the Virgin Mary, but not that he was crucified. Instead, they believe that he was taken away by God, who left a shadow in his place, and that Jesus will return one day at the end of the world. Unlike either Jews or Christians, they believe that Mohammed was God's last prophet.

"GOD IS GREAT!"

As in all Muslim countries, in Asia or Africa, Islam is a way of life for the people of Afghanistan. From childhood on, the Afghan is instructed by the mullahs (religious leaders) in the principles of the faith. Whether he becomes a herdsman or a farmer, the Afghan will always have a mullah in his village to read to him from the Koran to refresh his memory about the laws of Islam and the importance of keeping those laws sacred.

When a child is born, a mullah is called into the home to perform the first ceremony for the infant. The mullah says into the baby's ear, "God is great! God is great! I am a witness that there is no God but one God, and that Mohammed is his prophet! God is great! God is great!"

The ceremony, according to the Islamic article of faith, makes the infant a Muslim.

As a Muslim, the Afghan's entire life is governed and directed by the laws and tradition of Islam. The Koran not only prescribes the proper manners and times for worship, but also

*The Masjidi Jami mosque in Herat stands on a
site that has been a place of worship for various
faiths since the sixth century before Christ.*

gives the Muslim all the rules required for correct Muslim behavior.

Everything from the education of a Muslim to the proper conduct of women is prescribed in the Koran. The laws of business transactions as well as the judgment of legal, and even criminal, cases is directed by the words of the Koran.

This strict observance of the Islamic law, which pervades the life of the Muslim, has played a large part in keeping modern western influences weak in Afghanistan and other Muslim countries. But this keeping of the Muslim faith has also proved to be a strong bond. The people of Islam, in whatever country they live, tend to unite to defend each other and to fight together for each other's purpose. The oil boycott by the Islamic nations in 1973, to punish the United States for befriending Israel in its war against Egypt, is an example of Muslims' loyalty to each other and Islam.

To the very end, Islam and its holy book, the Koran, are evident in the world of the Muslim. When a Muslim dies, someone sits near his body and reads from the sacred book. An Islamic prayer is said before the bier is lifted. If a person meets the funeral procession, he is obliged, by Islamic law, to join the procession for at least forty steps, saying an Islamic prayer for the dead.

The deceased is placed in a grave in a manner that will have him face Mecca, birthplace of the prophet, when he is wakened by the trumpet of Judgment Day. There is more reading from the Koran before the mourners leave the cemetery.

Still, Afghans are not without superstitious practices. And for the most part these practices, and beliefs as well, are accepted in the Muslim faith as unsinful.

To protect themselves against evil spirits, Afghans resort to charms and spells, which mullahs often provide for a price. Charms are also used to cure illness. Spells are used to turn away the "evil eye," or to bring about something desired.

To look at the moon, on the third night of a new moon, is to bring bad luck. An itching right hand brings money. One avoids walking in front of a black cat. A woman, carrying an unborn child, does not touch her body during an eclipse, or else the child will bear a mark on the part of the body touched. Nor does she hold a knife during an eclipse, or else the child will be born scarred.

Whatever their superstitions, however, nothing changes their devotion to Islam. It is the force of Islam in their lives that has so often united them in the past against a common enemy. It is the force of Islam that has created the army of guerrillas that has been fighting the communist governments of Afghanistan, and, more recently, the Soviet Union's soldiers, tanks, and planes.

TRIBAL CUSTOMS

Tribal life is governed almost completely by unwritten tribal laws. Children are taught these laws as soon as they are able to understand them, and the laws soon become part of their personality. Pushtunwali, or the tribal laws of the Pushtuns, are the most important tribal laws in Afghanistan. We don't know where these laws originated or how old they are, but they fix the conduct of the Pushtuns as a tribe and the relationship of each tribesman to the rest of his people.

If a man does not pay a debt, his creditor may seize something valuable from the debtor, even a member of his family as prisoner, until the debt is repaid. The Pushtuns call this *barmateh*. In a dispute, the weaker man or men send representatives to the stronger with apologies. This process is called *nanawati*.

The need to avenge a wrong is very strong with the Afghans. This is called *badal*. If a member of a family is killed by another family, the killing must be avenged, even if it takes years, by a second killing.

A Pushtun considers nothing more shameful than the breaking of a promise (*ahd*). Pride and dignity, truth and sincerity are paramount in the life of the Afghan.

Hospitality (*milmastia*) is an essential part of Pushtun life. Every village has a guest house (*hujrah*) close to a mosque, fitted out with a stove or fireplace and a number of beds. "Welcome! May God bring you here always!" is the traditional greeting of a guest. The children bring food and attend the guest's needs. In the morning, the guest is greeted with a pot of hot milk and a loaf of bread.

Children, early on, are taught these and other courtesies. They are also taught to be courageous and to withstand pain. Instead of fairytales, they are told the stories of great fighters and heroes. Young boys are taught how to use a rifle and a sword.

The sword is most important in Pushtun tribal tradition. Swords are handed down from father to son. If a father dies in battle, the son raises the sword after him, and the widow is not expected to weep. Afghans have a deep respect for those who die on the battlefield, but a man who is killed while running away from the battlefield will be buried without ceremony.

In settled communities, villages, towns, and cities, certain laws of Pushtunwali are no longer honored. Here the Afghans carry guns only for hunting or on holidays. The village *malik* (chief) settles disputes that are not brought to court. Children are taught to be obedient and respectful rather than independent and courageous.

Most laws of Pushtunwali, however, still govern the attitudes and customs of Afghans wherever they live.

Cooperation is more important than competition. The duties of the son to his father, of the father to son and to others of his extended family are well understood and carried out. The

Pushtun dancers and musicians
perform at a festival outside Kabul.

relationship between landlord and tenant, employer and employee, teacher and student, are also well fixed, each giving the other proper respect.

Much regard and meaning is given to friendship. "When you shake a man's hand, you should remember him as long as you live" is a Pushtun saying. Generosity is considered an element of friendship. If a man has enough money to live on, he is expected to give money to those who have less. Giving gifts is a common practice, but the Afghan expects a gift of the same value in return. And friend is expected to stand up and fight for friend.

Emotions must be controlled, according to Pushtunwali. Men do not cry, except in the case of death. An angry man doesn't shout; he insults with words, quietly. If a fight does break out between two men, the battle is quickly ended if there are any friends around to stop it. Even in the writing of poetry, where the Afghan deals with all human emotions, feelings are concealed in carefully chosen words.

TRIBAL GOVERNMENT

The leader of a tribe is called the *khan*. He is usually a member of the most aristocratic family of the tribe. Sometimes he is an autocrat, the sole voice of authority in his community. However, even the most autocratic khan, assembling his clan to give them the orders of the day, will send his own employees to help farmers who need the aid. And in the evening, he will eat with his men in his own courtyard, after which he will sit down with them to talk or listen to his radio. It is the khan who settles every complaint, every difference among his people.

In many tribes, however, the common people have much to

say about their work and how they are governed, and insist on settling their own disputes in council (jirgah). They also guard the right to elect the khan in jirgah, to oust him if they are dissatisfied, and to decide on the length of the khan's tenure in office.

In the villages, the *malik* is the chief community official, elected by the villagers to his position. The malik settles disputes, collects taxes, and entertains guests at his own expense. Watchmen and village guards are elected by some villages, too, to protect the people from thieves, who may rob a villager of some of his household goods or crops that have yet to be harvested. Thieves almost never touch the villager's livestock because the owner marks his livestock with a recognizable dye.

WOMEN

Women in Afghanistan are second-class citizens. They have made some progress toward equal rights in the larger cities, but Muslim law and tradition make that progress painfully slow.

Young boys help their fathers in painting the house and clearing snow from the roofs; they never work in the house. Young girls help their mothers. Boys play all sorts of outdoor games, while the girls play with dolls. Until they reach the age of ten, girls may join with the boys in play, but once they are ten, they are no longer allowed that privilege.

Until recently, the only education girls received was at home. It wasn't considered necessary for a girl to know how to read and write. The number of girls in school has been increasing with the years, but slowly.

There is no such thing as dating between boys and girls in

the Western style. Marriages are, for the most part, arranged by parents, with or without the consent of the children. Marriages between cousins, but not of the same household, are preferred. But contact between young men and women, even those who are betrothed to each other, is always maintained at a distance. In the cities, boys may meet girls outside school, walk them home, telephone, and write to them. It is advisable for them, however, not to meet secretly. If such meetings were discovered, the girls particularly could incur grave punishments.

Sometimes a girl is contracted to be married when she is no more than twelve years old and her groom-to-be fifteen. Girls marry when they are sixteen or eighteen. At their weddings, in a ceremony conducted by a mullah, they are separated from their grooms by a curtain. Following the ceremony, the men leave with the groom for the groom's house. The women bathe and dress the bride and, at dawn, a ceremonial procession takes her to her husband.

The married woman does not leave her house without the permission of her husband. She never visits alone, except the home of her parents. Very few attend sports events or go to the theater.

In 1959, women were encouraged to remove the veil they have worn for centuries, and to some extent they do walk about with their faces uncovered. But even in the cities, such women wear a light shawl over their heads when they are out on the streets.

Still, women are not entirely subservient to their husbands. They do help decide family matters in the home and, by influencing their husbands, maintain a certain authority outside their homes.

[33]

The wife of a khan, or chief, in certain tribes, makes herself responsible for all the other women in her clan. At one time, tribal women attended to the equipment of their fighting men. A woman might pick up a gun and take part in the fighting.

There is considerable resistance to change in the role of women in this Muslim country. The Afghan constitution of 1964 gave women equal status. Some women now work in radio stations, as airline attendants, as nurses, in canneries and in weaving plants, but they are very few, and constitute only a small percentage of the Afghan work force. In Kabul, the police are ordered to protect instead of arresting women who do not wear veils.

Equal status comes slowly where tradition is so determinedly opposed to it.

EDUCATION

The 1931 constitution of Afghanistan decreed that education was compulsory for all Afghan children. Yet, only about 10 percent of the country's population is literate, the great majority of that 10 percent men and boys. The faith, traditions, and working habits of the people, despite their respect for learning, are largely responsible for this condition.

The mullahs among nomadic tribes teach the tribesmen the laws of Islam and how to write their names; and no more. In the villages, the mullahs do more. They set up classes in the mosques and teach young boys reading, writing, and arithmetic, as well as sections of the Muslim holy book, the Koran. The government may provide textbooks, writing materials, and desks, but the schools are largely funded by the village people. Schools set up by the government in these farming villages devote four hours a week to religious education during the first six years of schooling, a little less in the later years. The number of students in secondary schools, however, is comparatively small. Secondary schools are found only in the larger towns and cities, and they are not too well attended.

Many villagers oppose education beyond the elementary level. They are afraid that too much education may temper the religious enthusiasm of their children. They consider the young men, coming back from schooling in the cities, in western dress, with no turban on their heads, infidels.

About 85 percent of the population lives in rural areas, and older boys are needed on the farms to till the fields, harvest the crops, and take care of the sheep. As a result, attendance in school is irregular at best, and too many of these boys don't attend school at all.

For years much effort has been spent in attempts to improve the situation. Not only has there been increased funding of education in the country, but the curricula in the schools have been widened, moving them far beyond the limits of mullah teaching.

As early as 1907, schools, patterned after the schools of Europe, were established and teachers brought in from India. Later there would be French, German and, for a while, American teachers, too. By degrees, in addition to reading, writing, arithmetic, and religion, geography, history, science, handicraft, agriculture, and physical training were added to studies in the elementary schools. In the middle schools, the study of Persian, Pushtu, Arabic, and foreign languages, as well as mathematics, chemistry, physics, biology, and economics was added. At the older levels, students are prepared for college and university.

And all this schooling is free. Even the boarding of students who have to leave their villages and live in the towns and cities is often free.

There are schools for teacher-training, agricultural schools, schools for commerce and business administration, mechanics and technology. There are schools for law, medicine, political science, and engineering. Unfortunately, these schools are attended by only the tiniest fraction of the population.

Before the Soviet invasion, the government spent 10 to 14 percent of its budget on education, but many problems remain.

There isn't enough money to build all the schools needed in all the remote villages of Afghanistan. There aren't nearly enough libraries in the country, and there is a shortage of books, desks, and writing materials. A great need for teachers exists, but since teachers are very poorly paid, it is hard to recruit the number needed.

While the situation does improve, slowly, the percentage of girls and women attending all these schools in Afghanistan is miserably small.

HEALTH

hough the Afghanistan government has a continuing health plan, tuberculosis, typhus, dysentery, and other communicable diseases still ravage the country. Unhygienic practices, particularly in the rural and mountain areas, coupled with poor diet are responsible in a large measure for this continuing problem.

Muslims—and 99 percent of Afghanistan's people are Muslim—pay much attention to their personal cleanliness because their religious beliefs call for it. They wash their faces, hands, forearms, and feet before saying their prayers. Most Afghan men bathe their entire bodies before their morning prayers, particularly on religious festival days or weddings. There are public baths in the cities and in most towns, where men and women bathe with their friends, with separate rooms for men and women, of course. In the rural areas, men bathe in the streams and rivers. Women in these areas take their baths at home. City people use toothbrushes and toothpaste to clean their teeth.

Country people use a lather they create by crushing twigs from trees and bushes. Their white baggy trousers, along with their other clothes, are washed regularly, usually on rocks in a river. City people wash their laundry at home or send it to laundries that take the clothes out of town to be scrubbed on river rocks.

While the wealthier people of Kabul have modern bathrooms, the people in smaller towns have primitive bathrooms at best. Human waste is in evidence in alleys throughout the towns, and almost everywhere in the villages, where the winds blow the dust of human and animal wastes in all directions.

Only a few towns have water that is safe to drink. Very few towns have any organized way of disposing of waste materials. Both villagers and townspeople use water from open irrigation ditches for washing themselves, their food, their clothing, and for drinking. These ditches are polluted with the contamination of the soil. Unclean water is responsible for any number of intestinal diseases, eye disorders, and other sicknesses.

With only one doctor for about 40,000 people, there are not nearly enough doctors, nurses, or hospitals. In past years, the government has concentrated on training medical aides, assistant nurses, assistant dentists, and vaccinators. Malaria has been practically eliminated by teams of trained malaria inspectors and teams of vaccinators, and injections of vaccines and serums are regularly given to army recruits, factory workers, and even to those people living in remote areas of the country. In addition, the government has an ongoing plan of health education, by means of radio, films, pamphlets, newspaper and magazine articles, and freely distributed calendars. It also has instituted a number of rural development projects to bring sanitary conditions to rural districts.

But, despite efforts to educate the people on how to prevent and cure diseases, great numbers of Afghans are captives of old, traditional practices. When they fall ill, they often go to a mullah for advice. If an Afghan has suffered a snake bite, he will call on an herbalist, a man who believes that herbs can cure any kind of illness.

A traditional method to bring down a high fever is to rub the patient in flour, then wrap him or her in a goatskin. Animal skins are also worn around injured arms, legs, hands, or any part of the body that has been injured to affect a cure.

People in the larger towns and cities are moving away from these kinds of medical treatment. But a great part of the Afghan population lives in smaller towns and villages, and in remote areas of the mountains. These are the people who need educating and proper medical attention most, and are the hardest to reach. Tradition dies very slowly with people who are so far away from the mainstream of present-day knowledge and life.

Good diet is essential to good health, and the diet of most Afghans is far from good. Though Afghanistan has never experienced famine, a great number of its people live on a very limited diet and come close to starvation in the harsh winters.

Mud and brick houses in the city of Herat. Medical and social advances are slow in coming to Afghanistan, and primitive living conditions still exist in some cities as well as throughout most of the countryside.

Nomads have the best diet, as far as proteins are concerned. The sheep and goats they tend provide them with enough meat. For the rest of the people, however, meat is just too expensive.

Poultry, however, is reasonably priced. So are eggs. The other principal elements in the Afghan diet are grains, potatoes, milk, yogurt, butter, fruits, nuts and vegetables in season. In the winters, grain, potatoes, vegetables, fruits, and nuts are scarce, and the farmers have little money with which to buy anything else.

NATURAL RESOURCES, AGRICULTURE, AND INDUSTRY

There are coal and copper deposits in the mountains of Afghanistan, as well as oil, natural gas, sulphur, and some gold and silver. But due largely to transportation difficulties, these resources have been scarcely touched. There is no rail service in the entire country and roads are difficult to drive over because of their high altitudes, heavy snows, narrow rock gorges, and the hot and dusty deserts. The road to Herat from Kabul, for example, moves through high mountain passes, where there is always danger of sudden, killing avalanches. The road north of Kabul to the northern provinces climbs to an altitude of 9,800 feet (2,940 m), goes through a pass that has been blasted out of a perpendicular gorge, and crosses a river seven times. All this must be encountered to travel no more than 46 miles (74 km) along this road.

The difficulties in transportation, of course, increase costs so much that it is almost impossible for Afghanistan to compete with other producers of similar mining resources. The high costs and poor marketing conditions discourage investment in mine operations as well. Nevertheless, Afghan mining activities have increased in recent years, if only for domestic needs.

Coal is mined north of the Hindu Kush, in Kar Kar, in Darra-i-Suf, Ishpushta, and there has been some mining in the Southern Helmand Valley. There has been some drilling for petroleum in the Shirbarghan region. Copper, silver, lead, and zinc are mined in the Hindu Kush and in the northeastern mountain ranges. Lapis lazuli is mined in the Kokcha Valley. Gypsum and limestone, used for cement, and brick clay are found in a number of Afghan provinces. Potassium chloride and magnesium chloride, both valuable to industry, are also plentiful. Gold is panned from river sand.

There is really no lack of mineral resources in Afghanistan. What the Afghans lack is the money to build better roads to reach these valuable resources.

AGRICULTURE

There are no huge farms or great landowners in Afghanistan, where 96 of every hundred people are farmers or shepherds. The biggest farms are rarely larger than 50 acres (20 hectares) and the smallest about 5 acres (2 hectares).

On a number of the larger farms, there are sharecroppers and tenants. If the tenant provides only his muscle power, like a sharecropper, he is entitled to one fifth of what the farm produces. If he comes with his own farm tools, he collects one quarter of the produce. If he comes to the farm with his own animals as well, he gets half of the proceeds.

Some tenant farmers and sharecroppers live on the farms. Many live in villages nearby and travel to work on the land.

In addition to wheat and barley, the most important crops in Afghanistan are rice, millet, clover, sesame, cotton, tobacco, sugar beets, sugarcane, poppy, turmeric, and a variety of fruits and nuts. Cotton is grown chiefly in the Kataghan region and the Helmand province of Afghanistan. Silk, sesame seeds, and beet sugar are grown mainly in the northern areas of the country. Wheat is grown almost everywhere in Afghanistan, while the Arghandab Valley has the most plentiful fruit orchards.

The yield of the farmlands in Afghanistan, however, is limited, mainly because of primitive methods and tools for farming. There is also a problem with water.

The average rainfall for the country is low. Summer showers are rare in Afghanistan. The heavy rains come between October and April. Still the average annual rainfall is no more than 12 inches (30 cm). The farmers depend much on the melting of the snow in the high mountains to come down to the rivers, and the rivers to irrigate their soil.

Marshes build up on the land because of poor drainage systems. The poor drainage is responsible for the building up of soluble salts in the topsoil, destroying arable lands. Because there is a lack of rain for so many months of the year, the land hardens and breaks into hard clods.

Wiser farmers, particularly in the northern and western areas of the country, battle the water problems, and rather successfully, by diversifying their crops. They plant wheat, for example, only every two or three years. They alternate their wheat crop with barley or sugar.

There is little modern farming equipment in Afghanistan. Almost all the work is done by hand. The only aids most farms have are oxen to tread out the wheat harvest. Otherwise, they

[45]

still use an irrigation spade, a hand sickle, and wooden implements.

Before the Soviet invasion, the government, with American and United Nations help, had drawn up plans for irrigation and reclamation of arable lands. Some progress had been made in this area. The cotton yield in Afghanistan, for instance, has risen dramatically in recent years.

The nomads, who generally grow just enough crops to satisfy their own needs, nevertheless contribute considerably to the life and economy of the country. They supply milk, butter, and other dairy products for the diet of the Afghans, and wool for their clothing as well as for export. The hides of karakul sheep, most of which are raised by shepherds in the northern provinces of the country, bring much needed revenue into the country's coffers from abroad.

INDUSTRY

Afghanistan has no large industries. The potential for the hydroelectric power essential to industry on a major scale exists, but it has yet to be developed. There are, however, a number of developing small industries, such as wool mills in Kabul and Kandahar. There are cotton textile plants in the northern prov-

Primitive tools and agricultural methods, as well as a lack of rainfall, make farming a harsh and meager livelihood.

ince of Kunduz and in the eastern sector of the Parwan province. An important tanning industry manufactures water bags and bases for floating rafts out of goat and sheep skins. Kabul also boasts a match factory that produces about one quarter of a million matches every year, as well as a modern, mechanized bakery and a modern sawmill plant. Except for the cotton and cement industry, which are fairly well developed, all industry in Afghanistan is conducted on a rather small scale.

Children only eight and nine years old may be seen working in industrial plants. The child work laws are avoided by calling the children apprentices.

Almost every town has its carpenters, bricklayers, stonecutters, and blacksmiths. There are makers of fine furniture, carts, and carriages. The towns also have their tinsmiths, saddlers, and harness makers, as well as butchers, bakers, tailors, and other specialists.

In the bazaars, artisans and craftspeople have their own copper, blacksmith, and pottery shops to display their fine work.

Kandahar craftsmen string beads of chrystallite, for which they have a good and steady market in India and Mecca. The town of Istalaf is famous for its pottery, both painted and unpainted. Charikar is famous for its silverwork and its pottery.

In addition, there is much weaving in the homes, done mostly by women and children. The designs of their weaving are ancient, passed on from generation to generation.

Guns, musical instruments, swords,
and bright cloth are all sold in
this small store in downtown Kabul.

[48]

A HISTORY
OF CONFLICT
AND VIOLENCE

Afghanistan's history, through
the ages, has been a history of invasion, conflict, and violence. Before recorded history, countless tribes moved into the country, so that no one can say with certainty who lived in Afghanistan originally. There were the Uzbeks, the Turkomans, the Tajiks, among many others, and the Pushtuns who were to eventually become the dominant people in Afghanistan.

Then came the conquering Persian armies of Cyrus the Great and Darius the Great, dividing the country into seven different kingdoms.

After the Persians, came Alexander the Great and his Greek armies. After the death of Alexander, Afghanistan was constantly defending itself against the attacks of the Parthians from northern Iran, the Seleucids from Mesopotamia, and the Indians from the south.

Invasion after invasion kept Afghanistan in a turmoil. When the country was not fighting invading armies, the small kingdoms that made up Afghanistan were fighting among themselves for power and territory.

[50]

The Chinese invaded the country at the end of the seventh century. The Arabs were in control of Afghanistan in the tenth century. Turks ousted the Arabs, to be driven out by Genghis Khan and his Mongol hordes. After the death of Genghis Khan, came the conquering Tamerlane. Another horde of conquerors was led by a descendant of Tamerlane named Babur (the lion).

After Babur's death, Afghanistan became a battleground in the wars between India and Persia for possession of its land. Iran controlled Herat and Sistan. The Indians controlled Kabul. Kandahar was sometimes Iranian, sometimes Indian. Battles and wars were constant, cities and territories taken, lost, and retaken in conflicts that lasted for two hundred years, until the middle of the eighteenth century.

It was during this time that the Pushtuns began to grow in number and power. They played one side against the other, the Indians against the Persians, then the Persians against the Indians, while they developed a military strength of their own. They even joined the invaders' armies and one, Ahmad Shah Sadozai, became a leading figure in the Persian army.

When the Persian king was assassinated by some of his own officers, in 1747, Ahmad Shah Sadozai seized the moment to lead his own strong army into Kandahar, where he had himself named ruler of all the Afghans.

Ahmad Shah made the title stick. He renamed himself Dur-i-Durran (Pearl of Pearls) and, by consolidating the tribes of the country, established modern, independent Afghanistan.

For all of Dur-i-Durran's achievement, however, Afghanistan had not seen the last of foreign invasions. Toward the end of the eighteenth century, several areas of Turkistan were lost to Bukhara (now a part of the Soviet Union). Territory in Afghanistan was lost to the Hindus of India and never regained. It was the effort to regain the city of Peshawar that brought about the first Afghan–British War, which lasted from 1838 to 1842. The Afghans were no military match for the British, but it took Britain four years to defeat them. For some years to come, though Britain did not take over the country, it exerted considerable influence over the domestic and foreign policies of Afghanistan.

RUSSIAN INTEREST

This was a time of British and Russian colonial expansion. The British were fighting for control of India while the Russians were moving down into Turkistan and Bukhara. Afghanistan, situated between the spheres of interest of the two great powers, became a strategic area for both the Russians and British.

The Russians sent a mission to Kabul, in 1878, to negotiate for a common policy for Russia and Afghanistan. The British countered, sending their own envoy. But the British mission was stopped by Afghan troops at the Khyber Pass, on the road from Peshawar to Kabul, the traditional route through which invading armies surged into Afghanistan from the east. As a result of this action, the Second Afghan–British War was started.

Again the Afghans were defeated. This time, at the Treaty of Gandamak, Britain demanded and got supervision of Afghanistan's foreign relations and maintenance of a British mission in Kabul.

But, the following year, 1879, the entire British mission in Kabul was murdered, leading to the Third Afghan–British War that ended with British occupation of the country. British troops left Afghanistan soon after, but not before they left behind an amir (king) they could trust to keep British interests safe from disruption.

To further ensure stability in Afghanistan and to deter any Russian ambitions in the country, the British managed to make some arrangements with Russia. The border between Afghanistan and Russia was agreed to in 1887. In 1888, the border between Afghanistan and Iran was settled. In 1907, the Russians and the British signed a treaty in which Russia declared Afghanistan outside its sphere of influence, and the British as well promised not to occupy or take any part of the country.

All was quiet for a while in Afghanistan.

In 1919, however, Afghanistan, banking on the war-weariness of the British following the devastation of World War I, sent its troops into India. Despite initial victories of the Afghans, the British were quickly in command. Afghanistan asked for an armistice. In the treaty of peace that ensued, however, the Afghans were able to establish their sovereignty and complete control of their own foreign relations.

A treaty of Afghan-Russian friendship followed quickly. But neither treaty marked the end of British and Russian involvement in Afghanistan's internal affairs.

In 1929, an Afghan rebel named Bacha Saqao, led a rebellion against Amanullah, king of Afghanistan, and the king was forced to abdicate his throne.

The Russians believed that the British were behind the scenes, engineering the rebellion for their own purpose. They countered by sending Russian troops, disguised as Afghans, into the country. With their aid, the rebellion was squelched and Bacha Saqao was executed. Sadar Mohammed Nadir, a cousin to

Amanullah, became king of the Afghans, only to be assassinated four years later, in 1933.

Mohammed Zahir Shah, his son, assumed the throne, but was virtually a prisoner of his uncles and cousins, the real rulers of the country. He was only nineteen years old when he became king.

It was not too long, however, before Mohammed Zahir was able to shake the influence of his uncles and cousins, and remove them from power. For forty years there was relative peace in Afghanistan. Zahir introduced constitutional reforms, gave the people more and more power in the government, and took his revenge on his uncles and cousins by banning all members of the royal family from politics.

He made one error. In 1973, he went off on a visit to Italy. While he was out of the country, Lieutenant-General Mohammed Douad, his brother-in-law, engineered a military coup. Zahir was deposed from his throne. Douad became the ruler of Afghanistan, proclaiming the country a republic, with himself as both president and prime minister.

Douad's control of the country lasted five years. In a 1978 coup, Douad was killed and Noor Mohammed Taraki became head of the government. Taraki was the leader of the Communist People's Democratic Party in Afghanistan.

This well-armed group of Baluchi tribesmen symbolize Afghanistan's legacy of conflict and violence.

Taraki denied that the coup he had engineered was a communist takeover, but his statement did not ease the fears among the Afghan Muslims that Taraki planned radical social and economic changes. For Afghan Muslims, as for all Muslims everywhere in the world, Islam is a way of life that dominates their every action, social or economic. It is completely opposite to the communist way of life, which is not only opposed to any kind of religious faith but tries to destroy it as well.

There were minor protests against communist rule among the Afghan Muslims that soon blossomed into full-blown rebellion. By March 1979, some eleven months after Taraki had taken power in Afghanistan, thousands of Afghans in Herat rose in revolt against the Taraki government. The rebellion lasted for several days but was finally defeated. It is estimated that 20,000 Afghans were killed in the revolt.

The defeat in Herat, however, did not halt the uprisings. By the fall of 1979, Taraki's prime minister, Hafizullah Amin, an Afghan communist especially favored by the Soviet Union at the time, had executed 2,000 and imprisoned another 30,000 people. Still, it was said, twenty-two of the twenty-eight provinces of the country were controlled by the rebels.

Rivalry for power developed between Taraki and Amin, but Amin was the man the Soviet Union preferred to see in power. In a palace shoot-out in September 1979, Taraki was killed. Amin, with Soviet Union approval, took over the reins of the Afghan government. Taraki's reign had lasted seven months. Amin's reign would be considerably shorter.

While Amin was a communist, he displeased the Soviet Union by refusing to take all the orders that came from Moscow.

He turned down the Soviet advice to negotiate a peace with the Muslim rebels. He demanded that the Soviet Union change its ambassadors to Afghanistan. He was even bold enough to reject an invitation to Moscow for talks about the Afghan situation.

Amin was too independent for the Soviet Union. Nor was Moscow pleased with Amin's inability to end the Muslim rebellion against his communist government.

On Christmas Day, the Soviets began a massive military airlift to Kabul. Within a few days some 4,000 to 5,000 Soviet soldiers with artillery and armored vehicles landed in the capital city. The Soviet Union said, and continues to say, that their troops had been asked to come to Kabul by the Afghan government. Yet, on the Thursday after Christmas, Amin and a number of members of his family were summarily executed "for crimes against the people and the Afghan nation."

Babrak Karmal, with Soviet tanks and combat troops in fighting stance in Kabul, became the third communist president of Afghanistan. But, if anything, the Soviet invasion served only to reinforce the purpose and determination of the Muslim rebels.

The Soviets sent more combat troops and tanks into Afghanistan. It is estimated that there are some 95,000 Soviet troops in Afghanistan today. The troops and tanks fanned out all over the country. But the people's resistance to the invasion continued.

Afghans took to the caves and rugged mountains to conduct guerrilla warfare. They moved into Pakistan to buy arms, then returned to join the fight against the Soviets. Their forces were increased by soldiers who deserted the regular Afghan army to join the rebels. They cut communications between invading forces by taking over key roads and junctions. They attacked and took control of strategic towns and cities. What the Soviet Union had perhaps thought would be an easy victory has turned out to be a bloody and perhaps disastrous adventure for Moscow.

The General Assembly of the United Nations passed a resolution condemning the invasion and demanding that all invading troops be withdrawn from Afghanistan immediately. The United States stopped the shipment of grain, other than that already committed, to the Soviet Union, grain that the Soviet Union needs badly, as well as phosphates and other fertilizers. The United States also stopped sending high-technology materials to the Soviet Union, and cut down on its fishing rights in American waters. It also declared a boycott of the Olympic Games in Moscow.

While the United States acted alone, it called on all other nations to support its actions, designed to condemn the Soviet Union for its act of aggression and to demand its withdrawal from Afghanistan. And a number of nations followed the lead of the United States.

On May 14, 1980, a special meeting of defense and foreign ministers of the North Atlantic Treaty Organization (NATO) condemned the Soviets for their invasion and called on the Soviet Union to remove all its troops from Afghanistan. "The people of Afghanistan," the ministers declared, "must be free to shape their future without outside interference."

Today, Russian troops and tanks still occupy Kabul, Kandahar, and other major cities in Afghanistan, and are spread throughout the country. It is likely that, despite world condemnation, they will stay there for a long time.

The Afghans will not lay down their arms meekly. Whether the Afghans will ever regain control of their own country, however, without interference or domination by the Soviet Union, is, at the moment, a question that cannot be answered.

FOR FURTHER
READING

Bibby, Geoffrey. *Four Thousand Years Ago*. New York: Knopf, 1962.

Dupree, Louis. *Afghanistan*. Princeton, N.J.: Princeton University Press, 1973.

Lewis, Bernard. *Islam and the Arab World*. New York: Knopf, 1976.

Poullada, Leon B. *Reform and Rebellion in Afghanistan*. Ithaca, N.Y.: Cornell University Press, 1973.

Toynbee, Arnold J. *A Study of History*. New York: Oxford University Press, 1967.

Weston, Christine. *Afghanistan*. New York: Scribners, 1962.

Wilber, Donald N. *Afghanistan*. New Haven, Conn.: Human Relations Area File, 1962.

INDEX